Original title:
The Hallway of Hope

Copyright © 2025 Creative Arts Management OÜ
All rights reserved.

Author: Liam Sterling
ISBN HARDBACK: 978-1-80587-015-9
ISBN PAPERBACK: 978-1-80587-485-0

Illuminated Avenues

In a corridor bright, where shadows play,
We stumble on dreams like kids at a fay.
Each lightbulb a star, each echo a laugh,
We dance like we're quirky, no need for a path.

A sign that points left, then right, then back,
We giggle at choices, no sense to the lack.
With socks full of snacks, we march on with glee,
In a hallway of wonder, just you and me.

The Threshold of Change

At the edge of the room, a strange door appears,
It squeaks like a puppy, instilling no fears.
A doorknob that wiggles, just begs for a turn,
And each twist brings a giggle, oh how we yearn!

What's on the other side? Is it pizza or pie?
Perhaps dancing llamas or a pie in the sky?
With each hesitant step, we brace for the change,
Yet all we discover is a cat with a strange.

Whispers of Tomorrow

In tomorrow's whispers, we spy a few clowns,
With polka-dotted shoes and oversized frowns.
They juggle our dreams while sipping on stew,
And offer us candy, like it's something new!

Each giggle a promise, each snort a delight,
As we stroll down the hall, everything feels right.
A map made of giggles, a quest for the smile,
In these playful moments, let's linger awhile.

Echoes of a Sunlit Path

With echoes of laughter dancing in air,
The sunlight guides us, like a magical flare.
We bounce off the walls, with a hop and a skip,
In this corridor bright, we can't help but trip!

A squirrel in a tie, shakes hands with a broom,
Together they create an uproarious boom.
With each sunny step, we skip and we sway,
In our funny adventures, come join us and play!

Daring the Dark

In shadows we dance, with glee so bright,
Knocking on doors, hoping for light.
Monsters might lurk, in corners they hide,
But we've got a flashlight, come take a ride!

Socks without partners, we'll brave the unknown,
With goofy expressions, our fears overthrown.
Laughter like thunder, it fills up the space,
In darkness we find, a wild, silly place!

Shimmering Threads of Fate

Life's weaving a tapestry, bright and absurd,
With thread made of giggles, and laughs blurred.
Spinning the future, with colors so bold,
A quilt of our dreams, in each stitch behold!

When fate throws a curve, it's a dance we shall lead,
With pratfalls and flops, but yes, we succeed.
The fabric of destiny, an outfit so grand,
We strut down the path, like it's all just a band!

Paving the Way to Tomorrow

With bricks made of laughter, we build our grand way,
Each step is a chuckle, come join in the play.
Wobbling and giggling, we skip with such flair,
Tomorrow's a canvas, we paint with no care!

Our shovels are spoons, digging dreams with delight,
Mixing up futures, in the daytime's bright light.
With every small stumble, we cheer with a grin,
Paving our journey, where silliness wins!

Surging Beyond Stagnation

We're bouncing like rubber, with no place to rest,
In a pool full of chaos, we're all at our best.
Floating on laughter, just paddling along,
Who knew that in waiting, we'd find such a song?

Breaking the silence with joy so profound,
Like ducks on a pond, quacking all 'round.
Each ripple we make sends the worries afar,
Surging through life, we're our own silly stars!

The Doorway of Desire

In a lobby full of dreams,
Just got lost in a scheme.
Tripping over my own feet,
This desire's quite a feat.

A pizza slice for my heart,
It's all just a playful art.
With toppings of glee and cheese,
Life's too short for bad wees.

A door that swings, oh so wide,
Inviting all to have a ride.
Yet I clumsily fall through,
But hey, who needs a shoe?

Climbing ladders made of wishes,
Catch me in real silly dishes.
In this realm, my hopes arise,
Wearing dreams like funny ties.

Radiance in the Gloom

In shadows where the giggles hide,
Laughter sneaks out, nowhere to bide.
Glow worms dance with giddy glee,
In gloom, they welcome the spree.

A candle's flame, a wink in the dark,
Making jokes even the dogs bark.
Puns that flicker, oh so bright,
Turning wrongs into sheer delight.

Laughter glows like neon lights,
Chasing away the mini frights.
With every chuckle, I can see,
The radiance of sheer jubilee.

In the fold of misty nights,
Who knew gloom could start such flights?
With humor as my guiding star,
Comedy's never too far!

Beyond the Veil of Doubt

Peeking past the curtain's seam,
Where worries float like cream.
Doubt's just a funny scare,
Like socks with a picnic chair.

In a world where jests parade,
I trip and tumble, but I'm not afraid.
Wobbling on a teeter-totter,
Falling down? Just comedic fodder.

I charge at doubts with a grin,
With a rubber chicken under my chin.
Every question becomes a quest,
In this raunchy comedy fest.

Through the veil, a spark shines bright,
Making doubts seem like a flight.
With laughter lifting my spirit high,
Who needs wings? I'll just fly!

The Memory Lane

Wandering through a maze of yore,
Tripping over what came before.
Memories dance in quirky shoes,
Each stroll's a comedy news.

Recalling gigs and silly pranks,
Mixing giggles with the thanks.
I trip on a joke and recall,
Laughter makes us all stand tall.

Pictures stuck like silly glue,
Nostalgia's about the funny too.
Each twist of fate a made-up tale,
In this walk, I gladly sail.

In the lane, I laugh and play,
Every mishap leads to a yay!
Memories line the walls with cheer,
Turning past woes into quirky year.

Silence Before the Break

In shadows deep, I hear a sigh,
A rubber duck just floated by.
The waiting game, a funny jest,
Who knew that dreams could wear a vest?

Lonely socks in corners dwell,
Whisper secrets they won't tell.
A penguin waltzes through the door,
I laugh until I can't no more.

The clock ticks loud, a comedy,
It dances quite spectacularly.
But just before the punchline drops,
I slip on banana peels, and flop.

Tides of Transformation

Waves of change, they joke and tease,
A surfer falls and steals the breeze.
Flip-flops fly like birds in flight,
With sandy toes, we greet the night.

Seagulls squawk, they're in on it,
Cracking jokes that never quit.
"Surf's up!" they call, "Let's take a ride!"
While my drink spills, oh what a tide!

Transformation's just a laugh,
Like trying to divide by half.
A wave comes in, then I am wet,
Who knew the sea, my biggest pet?

Wings of the Unfettered

A chicken floats on clouds so high,
With dreams of flight, it dares to try.
I chase it down with spaghetti arms,
While it just giggles, full of charms.

Feathers in my hair, what a sight,
Dancing with the stars at night.
But owls throw shade on my grand plan,
It's hard to soar when you can't stand.

The freedom song, it starts to play,
A kazoo band joins and leads the way.
With wings so light, I jump and scream,
Life's just better when it's a dream.

The Breath of Fresh Beginnings

A gust of wind, it tickles me,
I sneeze so loud, the trees agree.
Spring blooms forth with a joyful shout,
While I trip on blooms, in and out.

Worms wear hats, what a sight to see,
They wiggle by quite joyfully.
"Plant a seed!" they chant so bright,
I plant my shoe; it's quite a fright.

Fresh starts are fun with mud and mess,
Each splat of dirt, I must confess.
But in the end, as sunlight beams,
I laugh aloud and chase my dreams.

The Sanctuary of Belief

In a room where doubts are banned,
Socks on the ceiling, dreams so grand.
Coffee spills, laughs echo loud,
Belief grows bold, wrapped in a shroud.

With flip-flops singing if you dare,
A pet iguana gives a stare.
The pizza box holds secrets near,
In this haven, we shed a tear.

Mismatched chairs in rainbow hues,
Who needs rules when we've got cues?
Jokes fly like kites in the air,
In this place, we choose to care.

So when the world feels weighty, dense,
Just grab a snack, and build the fence.
With laughter echoing to the skies,
Hope dances here, a sweet surprise.

Endless Horizons of Expectation

Beyond the door, the carpet's plush,
We set our sights with a joyful rush.
Expectations soar like butterflies,
In this land where giggles rise.

Cats in bow ties lead the way,
Letting us know it's time to play.
Unicorns parade, puns take flight,
Our hearts are light, our dreams ignite.

Bright banners wave with silly rhymes,
Tickling feet, we're lost in climes.
Here every moment's full of glee,
Hopes float like clouds, wild and free.

So take a joyride through this space,
With bubble gum smiles on every face.
The only rule? Just be yourself,
And dance a jig off the nearest shelf!

The Legacy of Dreams Unfolded

In the attic of old hopes and plans,
Dust bunnies dance, led by the fans.
Forgotten dreams in boxes stacked,
Remind us all, life's a bit whacked.

Jars of pickles line the way,
Each one holds a memory at play.
With each twist, a giggle comes out,
Life's endless jest, without a doubt.

A tuba sings, a banjo laughs,
While paper airplanes take their paths.
A world where laughter builds the frame,
And every mishap's part of the game.

So let's aspire with silly cheer,
Chasing shadows without a fear.
In this legacy, we all partake,
Building futures with every mistake.

Windows of the Heart

A window cracked, with a squeaky hinge,
The cat outside just gave a binge.
I peeked too quick, the curtain flew,
Now birds are laughing, what to do?

A heart so wide, it needs a screen,
To catch the dreams that hop and preen.
Flies and hopes are dancing floors,
While socks go missing—what's in store?

The windows smile, they wink and tease,
I wonder if they feel the breeze.
Inside my chest, the giggles grow,
Like jellybeans that overblow.

So here I stand, in awkward grace,
With silly thoughts on my old face.
A window view of life's sweet jest,
In this funny hall, I feel so blessed.

Reflections in Stillness

In a pond so clear, my face appears,
Bubbles rise like laughter through tears.
I make a face, the fish look back,
Do they judge me? I'll start a quack.

Reflections dance on lily pads,
With frogs who croak their comic fads.
Each ripple giggles at the clock,
Time's just a jester, wearing a smock.

The stillness hums its silly tune,
While tadpoles dance beneath the moon.
With every splash, a chuckle grows,
In playful waters, laughter flows.

So here I float, in silent glee,
As reflections wink and play with me.
In my own stillness, joy takes flight,
A funny mirror, pure delight.

Echoes of the Future

Time skips forward, a brisk little dance,
Echoes whisper, "Give life a chance!"
I trip on thoughts, hear laughter behind,
Is that my future? Oh, it's so blind!

In echoes bright, I hear the cheer,
Two squirrels debating who's more dear.
Will my tomorrow be wild like that?
With nutty dreams and a silly hat?

The future calls, a ticklish blip,
Promising giggles with every zip.
"Fasten your seatbelt!" it shouts with glee,
As I zoom past doubts, like a bumblebee.

So here I glide, on dreams set loose,
In echoes ample, I'll find my juice.
With laughter swirling around my fate,
What a fun year, it's never too late!

Searching for Brightness

With a flashlight dim, I roam the night,
Searching for brightness, what a delight!
I trip on shadows, let out a yelp,
Can't find the light? Well, that's just myself.

A glow-worm winks, "You look a bit lost,"
I blunder around, oh, what's the cost?
Searching for stars, I bump into trees,
They chuckle softly, "Find joy with ease!"

In every corner, I seek a beam,
Chasing bright giggles, what a sweet dream.
With lanterns swaying to a funny beat,
I shuffle along in big floppy feet.

So here I am, in the dark I roam,
Searching for brightness, a silly home.
With laughter lighting this winding path,
I embrace the darkness, and join the laugh!

Shadows in Transition

In a hallway where shadows play,
Socks on my feet go astray.
I trip on a rug, laugh out loud,
The echoing giggles form a crowd.

The walls whisper secrets, oh so bright,
They giggle and wiggle, a comical sight.
A picture frame does a little dance,
As I waltz by, it joins the prance.

A door creaks open, a breeze flows in,
It teases my hair, whispers of win.
I shake my head, what a silly show,
The hallway's alive with a fun glow.

As I exit, I turn with a grin,
The shadows are laughing, inviting in.
They say, "Come back, bring some cheer!",
I holler, "Next time, I'll bring a beer!"

Windows to a Brighter Day

Behind the glass, the world's a play,
Sunshine giggles, come what may.
With a wink, the curtains rise,
The room erupts in joyful sighs.

Birds in costumes, singing sweet,
Bouncing around on little feet.
A cat rehearses for a grand show,
Twirling about, with a flamboyant glow.

Sunbeams juggle as I take a peek,
Marshmallow clouds begin to speak.
"Join us up here in sky high fun,"
I shout, "Hold on tight, here we come!"

Each window opens, a laugh breaks free,
In bright colors, we dance with glee.
The day is mine, just what I sought,
Life's a party; oh, what a thought!

The Bridge of Possibility

Across the bridge, oh what a sight,
Possibilities twinkle in the light.
A parade of ducks in bow ties stroll,
Waddling along, they play a role.

With every step, the wood creaks wide,
It seems like the bridge has got some pride.
A rainbow whispers, "Trust the leap!"
While I hold tight to my dreams, not sheep.

Underneath, the river giggles too,
Bubbles of laughter, a joyous brew.
Pebbles dance, as I skip on by,
They cheer me on, oh me, oh my!

I glance back at where I used to be,
And leap ahead, feeling so free.
The bridge winks, a friend so dear,
"Take a fun route, your path is clear!"

A Glimpse of Dawn

Dawn peeks in through sleepy eyes,
Coffee's brewing, a warm surprise.
The sun slips in with a goofy grin,
And lights up the mess I'm living in.

Pajamas still on, I do a jig,
The toaster pops up, doing a gig.
Cereal dances in the bowl with glee,
Squirrels outside plotting a spree.

Sunbeams tickle, fading the night,
Forcing my curtains to take flight.
Curtains get tangled, oh what a mess,
Yet each snarl feels like a fun test.

With a burst of laughter, I embrace the day,
Mistakes are welcome in this play.
A glimpse of dawn, with cheer, I say,
"Let's make this madness a joyful ballet!"

The Shimmering Threshold

In the corridor of dreams, we stray,
Chasing shadows, laughing all the way.
With slippers on our feet, we glide,
Over scatterings of giggles, far and wide.

The walls painted with colorful delight,
Whispers of mischief float in the light.
A disco ball spins, though it's just a light,
And we dance like we don't care, feeling bright.

Every corner holds a funky surprise,
A rubber chicken, you won't believe your eyes!
Laughter echoes in this joyful chase,
Where silliness has its own grand place.

So step through the arch with a skip and a hop,
This shimmering path will never stop.
With each little jig, let go of your strife,
In this hallway of jests, we celebrate life.

In the Wake of Tomorrow

In the morning light, we trip and fall,
Carrying dreams that are just too tall.
A muffin misjudged as a bouncy ball,
And laughter erupts—what a delightful sprawl!

Tomorrow whispers gently in our ear,
As we chase it down with no hint of fear.
With mismatched socks and funny hats,
We strut like peacocks, oh, imagine that!

Chasing the sun, we leap, we roll,
With each silly slip, we reclaim our soul.
In the wake of tomorrow, we'll always find
A humor-filled journey, oh so kind.

So laugh at the bumps, embrace every cheer,
For life is but a comedy—let's make that clear.
In mirthful paths, our hearts will play,
In the wake of tomorrow, come what may.

Anchors of Faith

In a sea of chaos, we cast our root,
Navigating storms on a silly flute.
With rubber ducks as our guiding light,
We sail through laughter, into the night.

Anchors made of giggles, solid and round,
With each wave of joy, our spirits abound.
A treasure map leads to fun's friendly face,
In the ocean of whimsy, we find our place.

Navigate through clouds of whipped cream,
And stumble on dreams, with laughter we beam.
Our ship may wobble, but fearless we stand,
In the rough seas of life, we hold hands.

Each giggle, a beacon, shining so bright,
In this dance of absurdity, we find our light.
So let the tides carry us to new shores,
Anchors of faith keep us laughing outdoors.

Beyond the Veil of Doubt

Beyond the veil, where the goofy things fly,
Jellybean monsters wave as they pass by.
With hiccups of joy, we leap through the mist,
Dancing with shadows, we dare to persist.

In a world of tickles and whimsical sights,
We bumble and tumble, fueled by delight.
Clowns juggle dreams, while we cheer and shout,
What a grand adventure, beyond the doubt!

Questions tumble like kittens in piles,
Each one giggling, crafting new styles.
In this odd kingdom, where silliness reigns,
We shed all our worries, break all the chains.

So frolic and play with a wink and a grin,
In this wacky realm, let the fun begin.
Beyond the veil, where laughter's the key,
We uncover the magic that sets us free.

Lighthouses in the Fog

In foggy halls where shadows creep,
Lighthouses blink, but still we leap.
With rubber boots and hats askew,
We chase the beams, in search of you.

Wobbly walls that sway and sway,
We dance around, come what may.
The laughter echoes, truly grand,
As we find treasures, hand in hand.

Misty dreams that float on by,
Like jellybeans that refuse to fly.
With every turn, a giggle waits,
In this funny maze, we find our fates.

So raise your lamp, embrace the jest,
For every stumble is a quest.
In this silly, foggy spree,
We'll find our way, just wait and see!

The Rising Tide of Belief

The tide rolls in, our hopes at play,
With surfboards made of dreams, hooray!
We ride the waves, both tall and small,
With splashes bright, we've got it all.

Each wave a whim, each foam a cheer,
We laugh so loud, we've Nothin' to fear.
On sandy shores, we build our castles,
With seashells, dreams, and joyful hassles.

As seagulls squawk and steal our fries,
We wave them off, and roll our eyes.
With every swish, our spirits soar,
In this tidal dance, we're never bored.

So bring your buoy, and come along,
In the rising tide, we all belong.
With laughter as our guiding light,
We'll splish and splash, till day turns night!

Fountains of Potential

In busy squares where water flows,
Fountains burst with giggles, who knows?
Each drop of joy, a playful tease,
Splashing dreams, if you please!

Dancing droplets in the sun,
Juggling joy, we're all in fun.
With every spray, our hopes arise,
In this silly splash, we touch the skies.

The pitter-patter, quite a tune,
As laughter dances like the moon.
We gather round, our spirits high,
In fountains bright, we'll leap and fly.

So fill your cup, and take a drink,
From laughter's well, we'll surely stink!
With every sip and joyous shout,
In potential's pool, we twist about!

Embracing the Rays

Sunbeams peek through clouds of gray,
We stretch our arms, let's seize the day!
With goofy grins and silly hats,
We dance around like playful cats.

The rays of light, they kiss our skin,
As we embrace what's found within.
With giggles bright and hearts so light,
In this sunny moment, all feels right.

Chasing shadows, avoiding gloom,
We twirl and spin, make room for bloom.
With every ray, a chance to play,
In our funny dance, we'll sway and sway.

So gather 'round, let laughter flow,
In warm embrace, our spirits grow.
With every giggle shared today,
We find our joy in every ray!

Light Beneath the Shadows

In a corridor where socks do flee,
I chase them down, oh woe is me!
Beneath the lights that flicker bright,
I giggle hard, then bolt in fright.

Dust bunnies dance, they know the drill,
I trip and tumble, yet can't keep still.
With every stumble, laughter grows,
What joy it brings, these silly woes!

The vacuum's roar, a monster near,
I brace myself, but never steer.
With every twist, I play the part,
This hallway game steals all my heart.

In shadows long, I find a friend,
A mop that mocks my every bend.
Together we dance, as laughter flows,
In this strange lane, the funny grows!

The Journey Beyond Silence

In the corridor, where whispers play,
I sneak around like it's my day.
Every creak, a joke does tell,
The walls giggle, oh so swell!

Caught in the act, I freeze and stare,
A shadow waits, but does it care?
It's just the broom, with bristles wide,
We share a laugh, and then we glide.

Footsteps echo, but who's to know?
These walls are filled with tales of woe!
Yet here I stand, a clownish stance,
As cobwebs wave, I make my dance.

So here we wander, in fits and starts,
A zany crew of dust and farts.
In this journey, laughter's our guide,
Within the quiet, joy does hide!

Steps Towards the Unknown

I tiptoe lightly, what's that sound?
The floorboards chuckle, I'm dancing round.
With each step made, my fears take flight,
This hallway's a circus, what a sight!

The cat's in the corner, plotting a heist,
While I'm the clown, and he's not so nice.
Every turn surprises my silly heart,
With shadows lurking, I play my part.

I bump my toe on the doorknob tight,
And laugh so hard, I can't see right.
In this strange place, absurdity reigns,
Every mishap jars my funny veins.

So onward I go, through twists and bends,
With laughter echoing, this never ends.
A journey of giggles, far from the norm,
In each step taken, a new laughter's born!

Threads of Promise

In this narrow path, I weave and twirl,
With threads of joy, watch my skirt swirl.
Laughter spills, a fabric so bright,
As I trip over my own delight.

The corners hold secrets, they wink and smile,
Inviting me, to linger a while.
With every step, I make a new friend,
A curtain rod, a door that won't bend.

I juggle my hopes, my dreams, and my shoes,
Painting the walls with giggles and blues.
Hilarity waits at every turn,
In this hallway of jest, where candles burn.

So come one, come all, let's spin a tale,
Where silliness reigns, and laughs prevail.
In threads of promise, we stitch our glee,
Together we wander, so wild and free!

The Stretch of Promise

In the corridor of dreams so wide,
Juggling jellybeans, I slip and slide.
Hope's a game of hopscotch—oh so bright,
Tripping on wishes, I laugh with delight.

Here I gaze at futures, quite absurd,
Penguins in tuxedos, funny as a bird.
A kite that flew too high just to tease,
Catches on clouds, with the greatest ease.

Each door I open brings a quirky face,
A dancing log that leads the merry chase.
Smiles are the tickets to this wild ride,
Clowns on bicycles, cannot be denied!

In this stretch where chances boldly twirl,
Sunflowers wear sunglasses, give a whirl.
I'll skip through laughter, let worries unfurl,
For hope's a circus, come join the swirl!

Wandering Through Uncertainty

On paths of puzzlement, I meander slow,
Dodging rubber ducks in a row.
Banana peels dance with shoes not tight,
Every step uncertain, yet somehow light.

There's a squirrel with goggles, he shows me the way,
Offering advice in a funny display.
Lost maps don't scare me, I'm brave not shy,
With a pie in hand, I might just fly.

A clock strikes two with a big ol' grin,
Laughing at my hairdo, as if to begin.
With every twist, a giggle pops out,
Spinning around, I whirl with no doubt.

In this maze of chaos, I find delight,
Writing my story under glittery light.
Though paths may twist in ways that confound,
Laughter's the treasure that's always around!

A Tapestry of Aspirations

We weave our dreams in a fabric bright,
Socks on our hands, a curious sight.
With crayons in hand, we sketch our desires,
Jumping through rainbows, fueled by our fires.

There's a cat in a top hat, playing charades,
Whiskers of wisdom in stylish cascades.
Chasing balloons, twirling out of sight,
A kaleidoscope world, merry and light.

Strings of ambition get tangled with glee,
Fish on roller skates say, "Join us, whee!"
In this colorful dance of what we wish,
Jumping jacks and jelly, oh what a dish!

So we stitch our dreams with laughter and love,
Creating a quilt that fits like a glove.
Every patch holds a giggle, a chance,
In this quirky tapestry, come join the dance!

Starlit Avenues

Beneath the stars on this whimsical street,
Dance with the comets, oh, what a feat!
Lollipop trees hum a delightful tune,
Moonbeams giggle, they'll join us soon.

Footprints like marshmallows fluff on the road,
While twinkling stars share humor bestowed.
Frogs in tuxedos croak trivia fun,
Leaping through life, we laugh and run.

A suitcase of dreams just rolled by fast,
With surprises inside, oh, what a blast!
We toss silly wishes to the evening sky,
For hope is a candy that never runs dry.

So dance in the moonlight, let your heart twirl,
On starlit avenues, watch the magic unfurl.
With giggles and dreams interwoven tight,
We find joy in this splendid night!

Whispers Between Doors

In the damp, dark corridor, we sneak,
Where the creaky floors sometimes squeak.
A sock behind the door, oh what a find,
Maybe it belongs to the ghostly kind.

Laughter echoes, silly jokes unfold,
About the haunted walls, stories told.
A napping cat somewhere takes a stretch,
While we plot mischief, who's gonna fetch?

Bouncing shadows dance like silly clowns,
Wearing mismatched socks and old, worn-down crowns.
The doorbell rings, but who could it be?
Perhaps it's just Tom, eating more than three.

With every turn, a giggle on the breeze,
As we twist and swirl, our minds at ease.
Who knew that empty halls could bring delight?
In this absurd space, we find our light.

A Corridor of Dreams

In a hallway bright with vivid hues,
Laughter spills and spreads like morning dew.
Where ceiling fans toss confetti up high,
And ticklish air makes the shy folks fly.

Dreams hang low on crooked hooks,
Like quirky outfits from old storybooks.
We giggle as we walk on rickety floors,
Creating puns and opening imaginary doors.

A rubber chicken lays beneath a chair,
It squawks a tune, oh what a rare affair!
With mismatched slippers, we dance through the mist,
Who knew in this madness, we couldn't resist?

Each echo here offers a chance to play,
With pranks and tricks brightening the day.
In the hallway of dreams, we find our scheme,
Navigating life, absurdity the theme.

Echoes of Tomorrow

Down the hall, where echoes tease the night,
Silly shapes bounce like a marshmallow fight.
Tomorrow's dreams prance on shoelace strings,
As giggles rise, the echoing laughter sings.

Here a snail races, wearing a cape,
Just watch, it's forming the next big shape!
A bouquet of socks, mismatched, afloat,
Vying for the title of funniest goat.

Whispers tell tales of a fridge that clucks,
A gopher in there that only cracks jokes.
We skip through the day, like candy in spring,
With echoes of tomorrow, oh what joy they bring!

The hallway hums with a magical breeze,
As we chase the ticks of the clocks with ease.
In a world where oddities happily dwell,
We step into laughter, a whimsical spell.

Paths Unseen

In paths unseen, we frolic and play,
With rubber ducks floating the silly way.
A twist here, a turn, what's that behind?
Oh, just a tuxedoed cat, one of a kind!

We gather the giggles like fallen leaves,
Floating and spinning through whimsical eves.
A prankster balloon, filled up with giggles,
Pops in the air, causing all the wiggles.

On shadowy waves, where the tickles start,
An armchair hums, it's a fine work of art.
Tea parties form with the cups that dance,
Who knew that this chaos could spark romance?

In the corners, the echoes bring clever sights,
Painted fairies wriggle through soft, silver lights.
On paths unseen, where joy never ends,
We find our laughter, in these silly bends.

Where Fears Meet Faith

In a corridor filled with dread,
A sock was lost, the truth unsaid.
Goblins dance around the bend,
But laughs arise, they too can mend.

A cat with flair, in slippers goes,
Chasing shadows, striking poses.
Fears take flight, like balloons in air,
As faith trots in, a silly bear.

With wobbly knees, we wade through gloom,
Like a piñata bursting, making room.
Embrace the chance, to take a leap,
Even if it ends in heaps!

So join the parade, let's not be shy,
With silly hats, we'll reach for the sky.
Where fears and laughter intertwine,
In this hallway, oh, what a time!

The Silent Invitation

A door ajar with whispers near,
Inside, a party brewed with cheer.
The silent call, it echoes loud,
Break out the treats, beneath the crowd!

A fish in a bowl, wearing a tie,
Invites us in, oh my, oh my!
With laughter ringing, the dance begins,
As rubber ducks sway, oh what a spin!

Forget the fears, the blunders too,
We'll toast marshmallows, just me and you.
In silliness we find our grace,
With every trip, we'll laugh and race.

So join the fun, it's never late,
In the hall of giggles, we're feeling great!
With every step, let worries sigh,
The silent invitation is nigh!

Bridges of the Heart

Building bridges made of candy,
Gummy bears and licorice dandy.
We stumble, trip, but who would care?
We're on a quest for chocolate fare!

Pineapple hats, and silly shoes,
Crossing over with nothing to lose.
With every giggle, the span grows wide,
In hearts we meet, take a goofy ride!

Wobbly beams and dancing lights,
Where laughter echoes, it ignites.
A bridge of joy, we all can share,
In silly antics, no fear, just dare!

So wave goodbye to serious schemes,
In the land of fun, we chase our dreams.
Let's build our path, with all our might,
On bridges of the heart, pure delight!

Embracing the Uncertain

In a world where penguins fly,
Bubble-wrap suits, oh my, oh my!
We tiptoe through a jumble of chance,
Laughter erupts, let's join the dance!

A pickle on pogo, what a sight,
Juggling dreams, oh so light!
With ups and downs, it's quite the ride,
In wobbly boats, we'll surf the tide.

The uncertain calls, a merry tune,
With dancing ducks beneath the moon.
We laugh, we trip; it's part of the game,
In squeaky shoes, we find our fame!

Embrace the chaos, let laughter reign,
In the circus of life, we'll break the chain.
So here's to risks, with giggles in store,
In uncertain seas, let's boldly explore!

The Untold Journey

Upon a wooden shoe we tread,
The path ahead, a cupcake spread.
With jelly beans for all our fears,
We laugh and dance through silly tears.

Through every twist, a rubber chicken,
With every turn, our giggles quicken.
The map we clutch, a doodle spree,
Adventure sings like bumblebees.

A cat in shades leads us astray,
While squirrels dance the night away.
Yet hope is like a gumdrop bright,
We'll find our way by pure delight.

In this parade of strange delights,
We twirl with dreams and fuzzy tights.
The journey's wild, but never grim,
With every step, we laugh, we swim.

Gardens of the Undaunted

In gardens bright where daisies bloom,
We plant our jokes, dispel the gloom.
A gnome who tells the funniest tales,
While butterflies wear tiny veils.

Each seed we sow with laughter's cheer,
Grows more than flowers, never fear.
With dancing weeds and jabbering bees,
We tickle roots and climb up trees.

A spaghetti vine, it twirls with grace,
While squirrels hold a nutty race.
In this green maze, we chase delight,
And giggle loud from morn till night.

With every bloom, our spirits soar,
In gardens kissed by humor's lore.
The sun above, a laughing friend,
In this strange place, we never end.

Reflections of a Brighter Day

In mirror worlds, we dance around,
With smiles flipped upside down.
A wink from shadows, oh so sly,
As rubber ducks go sailing by.

The sun's a grinning peach today,
Casting giggles every way.
Bouncing, leaping, all in stride,
With daffodils as our wild guides.

Puddles splash with silly glee,
As laughter ripples, you and me.
The wind shouts jokes, a whirlwind feast,
In this bright day, we are released.

With every glass, the world's a stage,
Where silly moments never age.
Reflections show we're bold and free,
In funny tales, our hearts agree.

Songs of Rebirth

In crooked notes, our voices blend,
A symphony that will not end.
With ukulele and a drum,
We tap our toes and hum along.

A caterpillar sings off-key,
While flowers clap in harmony.
We shimmy, shake, a wild bright scene,
With every step, a giggle sheen.

The sun, a jester in the sky,
Sends rays that make the shadows fly.
With every chord, the air gets light,
Our songs of life take wondrous flight.

In every note, new colors paint,
A canvas wild, no need to faint.
With laughter stitched in every seam,
We dance through life, a joyful dream.

Beacons of a New Dawn

In the morning, slippers dance,
Coffee spills, a clumsy chance.
Sunshine peeks through dusty doors,
Laughing at our morning chores.

Cats chase tails, a silly sight,
Dogs in pajamas, what a fright!
Laughter echoes, bright and clear,
Starting fresh, it's all good cheer.

A Journey Beyond Shadows

With socks that clash, we stride along,
Pajamas worn like a silly song.
Taking steps toward the unknown,
Tripping on dreams we've overgrown.

Goblins giggle in the mist,
Tickle fests we can't resist.
Wandering through life's funny maze,
Finding joy in the wildest ways.

Fragments of Light

Sunbeams peek through curtains wide,
A disco ball in the hallway slide.
Mismatched shoes on the floor reside,
In the laughter, we take pride.

Jellybeans dance on the table,
What a mess, but we are able.
Fragments of joy, strung like pearls,
In our hearts, the chaos twirls.

Unity in the Void

In the void, where giggles float,
Whiskers twitch on a silly goat.
Laughter echoes, fills the air,
Unity found in our wild hair.

Ticklish toes and playful sighs,
Chasing dreams as time just flies.
Together we'll plow through the fun,
Earning joy, one smile won.

The Long Walk to Renewal

I trod a path of dusty dreams,
With mismatched socks and silly schemes.
A rubber chicken guides my way,
As laughter bounces, brightening the day.

Step by step, my heart grows light,
Tripping over puddles, what a sight!
A dance of joy upon the floor,
Each giggle echoes, wanting more.

The ceiling fans all spin around,
Chasing giggles that know no bounds.
I slide on floors, arms open wide,
Embracing chaos, my funny pride.

At the end of this quirky lane,
I shed my doubt and all my pain.
With every step, a fresh new start,
And laughter bubbles from my heart.

Embracing the Unknown

On this journey where logic hides,
I wear a tutu and rollerblading slides.
The map is scribbled, crayon in hand,
As I twirl and leap across the land.

The shadows whisper, 'Dare to play!',
A cupcake beckons me to stay.
With one big bite, I take the leap,
Into the unknown, not a care to keep.

Balloons are tethered all around,
Floating high, defying the ground.
With a sassy wink, I greet the day,
In my butterfly wings, I'll find my way.

Every turn holds a silly surprise,
Like socks with polka dots that blind my eyes.
I welcome oddities with arms spread wide,
Embracing the unknown, my joyful ride.

Footprints in the Mist

Footprints squished in silly goo,
Leading off to places brand new.
With a rubber duck, I sail the stream,
Leaving trails that shimmer and gleam.

Every step is a ducky dance,
Spinning circles, a chance to prance.
The mist is thick with giggling glee,
I can't help but chuckle, oh what a spree!

A wobbly path filled with surprises,
Each squishy step, joy arising.
The world is bright, the sun does peek,
As laughter flows, cheek to cheek.

In this playful fog, I roam,
Each giggle whispers, 'Welcome home!'
Footprints of joy in every twist,
In this playful haze, how could I resist?

Shades of Courage

In a world awash with colors bright,
I wear my shades, oh what a sight!
A polka dot tie and glittering shoes,
Stepping boldly into each quirky muse.

With every leap, I twirl and sway,
Daring the doubts to get out of my way.
I juggle fears like a clown on stage,
Turning worries into laughs, an outrageous page.

Rainbows dance on my silly quest,
With courage wrapped in a bright vest.
I sing out loud, a goofy tune,
With hope as my winged balloon.

So here's to the brave, the silly, the bold,
In shades of courage, stories unfold.
I leap with zest into the light,
Finding the funny in every fright.

Threads of Light

In a corridor where shadows play,
A cat wears shades, it's here to stay.
The mice hold meetings, vote for cheese,
While lamps project a glow with ease.

A wall of mirrors reflects my hair,
I dance with edits—who needs a care?
The floor creaks secrets, the paint peels too,
But I still strut in my shoes of blue.

Lightbulbs flicker like disco lights,
The exit sign is giving fright!
I tap my feet to a ghostly beat,
This hallway's rhythm can't be beat.

A selfie stick is my best friend,
In this limbo where jokes never end.
I'll gather these laughs and call them gold,
In the hallway where I'm forever bold.

Seeds of Change in a Darkened Room

In a dark room, seeds start to sprout,
They're wearing hats and dancing about.
With every blink, they grow a bit,
Frogs jump in, all laughing—split!

A broomstick sweeps in with flair,
And stirs the seeds with such great care.
They toss confetti made of dreams,
Brightening up the darkest schemes.

Potatoes signed a contract, bold,
For reality shows that won't catch cold.
Carrots sport shades and a sigh,
While broccoli wears a tie, oh my!

An eggplant juggles, it's quite a sight,
In this room, change feels just right.
What happens next? A squirrel's the host,
With a megaphone and a buttered toast!

Paths of Endless Potential

On paths where laughter paves the way,
Each step's a joke—come out and play!
With every turn, the silliness grows,
Upside-down signs and clownish prose.

Pigeons wear helmets, a serious crew,
While kids ride unicycles for a view.
The sidewalk cracks spell out "giggle,"
Who knew that paths could make us wriggle?

Each corner leads to ice cream shops,
Where flavors leap and nothing stops.
Banana splits do the cha-cha slide,
And sprinkles parade with joyous pride.

So take a step, feel the delight,
In paths of potential, everything's bright.
With every giggle, the world spins more,
Let's dance through this whimsical door!

Horizons Beyond the Fade

Underneath the fading light,
A snail pops out to say, "What's right?"
With sunglasses on and a shell so fine,
It slimes across the finish line.

The sun tumbles down, but never cries,
It leaves us hints in orange skies.
Birds wear spectacles, look quite proud,
Singing tunes that draw a crowd.

"Chase your dreams!" the twilight shouts,
While cheese blimps float without doubts.
Hippos in suits dance with flair,
At horizons where laughter fills the air.

So, fear not the fade, embrace the glow,
In this land where silliness flows.
With every giggle, we gracefully blaze,
Creating new paths through sunset's haze.

Crawling Toward Clarity

On hands and knees I slowly creep,
Searching for wisdom, not a peep.
Thoughts tumble down like shoes on stairs,
Why do I trip on my own pairs?

A lightbulb flickers, oh so bright,
But it's just the fridge, late at night.
Am I the tortoise in this race?
Or simply lost in outer space?

Reality winks as I stand tall,
My knees are sore, but I'm not small.
Clarity sets in like a thick fog,
At least I'm moving; I'll take that log!

With every bump, my troubles fade,
Laughing at life, the grand charade.
Twists and turns will come my way,
But I'll keep crawling—come what may!

Shadows Giving Way to Glow

In corners dark where giggles hide,
Shadows dance like they've got pride.
They stretch and yawn, then start to play,
Are they my fears? Oh, go away!

A flick of light makes them retreat,
They tumble over tiny feet.
I crack a joke; they start to cower,
And then I laugh—a glowing shower!

With every chuckle, gloom takes flight,
My silly moves turn wrong to right.
A shadow slips, it trips on air,
I guess it didn't see me there!

Glowing hues now paint the room,
I chase away the sense of gloom.
Through laughter's bridge, they fade away,
In my bright world, they cannot stay!

Palettes of Possibility

Splatters of paint on my old shirt,
Mixing laughter with a touch of dirt.
Each stroke a chance to make it grand,
Or just a doodle—it's all unplanned!

Brush in hand, I feel so bold,
Dreaming in colors, bright and gold.
What if I splash on a purple whale?
Or a polka-dotted, singing snail?

With every stroke, my mind runs free,
Creating worlds that only I see.
The canvas chuckles, it's quite a tease,
It loves my blunders, they come with ease!

Possibilities sprout like wildflowers,
In my whimsical world of powers.
I paint my fate with every hue,
And giggle at all the things I can do!

The Highway of Heartbeats

I travel down a road of beats,
With every laugh, my heart skips fleets.
With potholes filled with silly songs,
And billboards with jokes that last so long.

A car zooms by, with music loud,
They wave a hand, I feel so proud.
The GPS says, 'Continue straight,'
But I take a detour—why hesitate?

Road signs point to 'Misadventure,'
With splashes of fun, it's a true censure.
I change lanes, wiggle and sway,
Through happy chaos, I'll find my way!

At every red light, I tap my feet,
With the rhythm of hope, life is sweet.
As every heartbeat thrum and race,
This highway of laughter's my favorite place!

Resonance of Renewal

In the corridor where dreams roam free,
A cat in a tux, sipping sweet tea.
With echoes of giggles and playful prance,
Who knew this hallway could throw us a dance?

A stack of old shoes, a hat made of cheese,
The characters here always aim to please.
A pogo stick jumps, a balloon takes flight,
We giggle and wiggle in pure delight!

Maps that lead nowhere, oh what a jest!
In this silly hallway, we feel so blessed.
A parade of oddities spins round and round,
Where laughter erupts, and joy can be found!

So gather your courage, don't shy away,
In this charming corridor, we all want to stay.
With wit and whimsy, we'll chase away gloom,
In the nooks of this space, there's always more room!

The Ascent of Courage

Up the stairs where mischief thrives,
A squirrel with glasses seriously strives.
With each wobbly step, we giggle anew,
A dance with the shadows, a whirlwind view!

There's courage in laughter, a skip in our heels,
As we face the great unknown with silly appeals.
A cupcake-shaped cloud gives us a wink,
Carried by whimsy, we soar and we sink!

An octopus juggles a dozen ripe pears,
While we cheer him on with our joyful, loud cheers.
The balderdash blossoms, the hilarity flows,
With every ascent, our bold spirit grows!

So shout to the stars, let your giggles collide,
In this uplifted journey, feel joy as your guide.
With a heart full of chuckles, we rise without fright,
Scaling humor's heights, we're all set for flight!

A Passage Through Time

In a corridor shimmering with sparkling light,
We travel through moments, both silly and bright.
A clock that runs backward, a dance that's a race,
In this wacky time tunnel, we quicken our pace!

Dinosaurs grinning in polka-dot hats,
Sipping tea with astronauts and their pet cats.
Each tick of the clock brings a new wacky twist,
Where laughter and fun are impossible to miss!

From the future to past, in our gleeful flight,
We bounce with delight, never losing our bite.
A flash of a jest as the seconds unfold,
This passage of time is pure joy to behold!

So gather your friends, let's skip through the years,
With humor our compass, we'll conquer our fears.
In this passage of laughter, we flourish and shine,
For every tick-tock is a reason to dine!

Reflections in Twilight

As the sun dips low, colors start to blend,
In a mirror of giggles, where silliness bends.
A rabbit that dances, a turtle that sings,
Twilight reflects all the joy that it brings!

With each fluffy cloud made of laughter and cheer,
Whimsical shadows appear and endear.
A jester's cap floats by, oh what a sight,
As we revel in humor, from morning to night!

The stars start to sparkle, with mischievous ease,
The moon pulls a prank with a giggling breeze.
In this twilight reflection, we bask in the glow,
Of a world full of joy, where bright spirits flow!

So let's dance with the dusk and sing with the stars,
In the reflections of twilight, we'll heal all our scars.
With laughter our lantern, we brighten the night,
In this whimsical realm, everything feels right!

The Unseen Bridge

In a corridor filled with dreams,
A cat walks by, plotting schemes.
It trips on shoes, slips on the floor,
But laughs it off and comes back for more.

Balloons are tied to every doorknob,
With messages that make you sob.
"Don't let the cat take the last slice!"
A giggle erupts, oh what a paradise!

The lights flicker, but no one cares,
Except for the mice with secret lairs.
They gather crumbs like bank deposits,
And throw a party with silly visors.

So if you trip, just dance it out,
Join the mice, and twist about.
In this hallway of whimsy and cheer,
You'll find the joy, year after year.

Voices Beyond the Door

Behind every door, there's a sound,
A chorus of laughs that can astound.
One door sings, another just hums,
With rhythm and beats that tickle your thumbs.

Puns fly high, like kites in the sky,
While grandmas argue about pie.
"It's too sweet!" or "Where's the crust?"
In this bizarre debate, we all trust.

A talking dog claims to solve math,
But when he tries, he goes off-path.
"Two plus two? That's a fetch, my friend!"
His crumpled papers, all around, they blend.

So knock on the doors and listen, my mate,
You may just find the world's best fate.
With voices of joy, the silly and bold,
These secrets of laughter are worth more than gold.

Upward Slopes of Change

Life is a hill with a wobbly sign,
"Walk like a penguin, you'll be just fine!"
And as you stagger, with arms opened wide,
You may just fall, but at least there's pride.

On the steps, there's a worm with style,
Wearing a hat, he's seen every mile.
"I'm the captain of this slippery way!"
Get up, he says, and join the parade!

Each stumble brings its own sweet flair,
Like an accidental split in midair.
Laughter echoes with each small mistake,
A symphony of giggles, make no mistake!

So sprint up that slope with ridiculous glee,
Become the star of your own comedy.
And if you fall, don't worry a bit,
Roll on like a ball, that's the best fit!

A Canvas of Tomorrow

In a corner where the colors collide,
A painter laughs, with nothing to hide.
Her brush slips and makes a weird splat,
"Is it modern art?" she asks the cat.

With strokes that create a scene so bizarre,
Dancing chickens, and a pink flying car.
"Why not?" she says with a wink and a beard,
Art is a journey, not meant to be cleared.

Spray cans pop with silly sounds,
As squirrels debate who losing their crowns.
"You splashed paint on my tail, you fiend!"
But all are laughing, as chaos convened.

So grab a brush, don't just stand there,
Splash your own dreams, throw them in the air.
For a canvas that tells the best of tomorrow,
Is painted with joy, no space for sorrow.

Steps of Resilience

In sneakers too big, I shuffle along,
Catching my breath in a sing-song.
With each awkward step, I giggle, I glide,
This journey's a dance, come take it in stride.

A banana peel waits, my fate to decide,
But I leap over it, and then I slide!
Resilience is silly, it makes me feel great,
Nothing can stop me, I'll dance with fate!

With shoes untied and pants astray,
I waddle down life in my own funny way.
Laughter is armor, and joy is my shield,
In this wobbly world, I refuse to yield!

So bring on the bumps, the falls, and the spills,
With chuckles and giggles, I'll conquer the hills.
In this clumsy parade, I'll find my sweet groove,
For every misstep helps me to move!

Corridor of Dreams

In dreams, I cartwheel through the air,
Bumping into rainbows, without a care.
The walls are lined with giggles and cheer,
Each doorway whispers, 'Adventure is near!'

I met a cat who wore a top hat,
He gave me a riddle, then ran off to chat.
A door swung wide, 'What's behind this fence?'
A unicorn shouted, 'It's all quite immense!'

Socks are sliding, my feet are a blur,
I dance with the lamps, give them a purr.
The hallway stretches, it twists and it bends,
Unraveling wonders where silliness blends.

So tiptoe through laughter, let joy take the lead,
In this corridor of dreams, let your spirit be freed.
Each step is a story, each corner a prize,
With smiles as our compass, discover the skies!

Lanterns in the Gloom

Flickering lanterns light up my bounce,
Casting shadows that twist and renounce.
A shy ghost whispers, 'Join me in fright!'
I offer a cupcake, and we share a bite.

Misty giggles fill the haunting air,
As we dance in the dark without a care.
Lanterns of laughter, oh how they gleam,
Painting the shadows with joy like a dream.

In corners I peek, find socks with a grin,
A sock puppet army just waiting to win.
They wave their long arms and shout out a jest,
In this gloom, laughter surely is best!

So when the night grows thick and the world feels too deep,
Bring out your lanterns, let laughter seep.
With lanterns in hand, through shadows we'll roam,
Creating our magic, together, we'll foam!

Passageway to Possibility

In this passageway, I take off my hat,
A raccoon in a waistcoat says, 'Fancy that!'
He juggles some acorns and spills them with flair,
While I'm busy dodging a cat doing air.

Each step is a riddle, each turn holds a tune,
A penguin in boots barrels past like a loon.
With a wink and a bow, he slides on a pie,
'Life's just a laugh!' as he wobbles bye-bye.

The walls sprout mustaches, they dance on their own,
Playing charades with a pole made of stone.
I'm caught in a twirl, a spin and a shout,
Where silliness reigns; let's wiggle it out!

So grab your spurs, let's leap and let's prance,
In this passageway, there's always a chance.
For life is a party, with laughter we fill,
Each twist and turn, a laugh to fulfill!

www.ingramcontent.com/pod-product-compliance
Lightning Source LLC
Chambersburg PA
CBHW070322120526
44590CB00017B/2785